[TULIP]

THEODORE JAMES, JR.

PHOTOGRAPHS BY HARRY HARALAMBOU

HARRY N. ABRAMS, INC., PUBLISHERS

For Jay Applegate and John Greene

EDITOR: Sharon AvRutick
DESIGNER: Helene Silverman
PRODUCTION MANAGER: Maria Pia Gramaglia

Library of Congress Cataloging-in-Publication Data

James, Theodore.
  Tulip / Theodore James, Jr. ; photographs by Harry Haralambou.
      p. cm.
Includes bibliographical references (p.   ).
  ISBN 0-8109-9099-7 (pbk.)
  1. Tulips. I. Title.

SB413.T9 J36 2003
635.9'3432—dc21

                              2002152729

Printed and bound in China

10 9 8 7 6 5 4 3 2 1

Harry N. Abrams, Inc.
100 Fifth Avenue
New York, N.Y. 10011
www.abramsbooks.com

Abrams is a subsidiary of
LA MARTINIÈRE
GROUPE

PAGE 1: FOSTERIANA TULIP 'RED EMPEROR.' PAGE 3: SPECIES TULIP 'LITTLE BEAUTY' AGAINST A
CARPET OF CREEPING THYME. OVERLEAF (CLOCKWISE FROM UPPER LEFT): VIRIDIFLORA TULIP
'SPRING GREEN,' KEUKENHOF GARDENS, RED EMPEROR TULIPS, DUTCH BULB FIELD.

CONTENTS

Anatomy of the Tulip

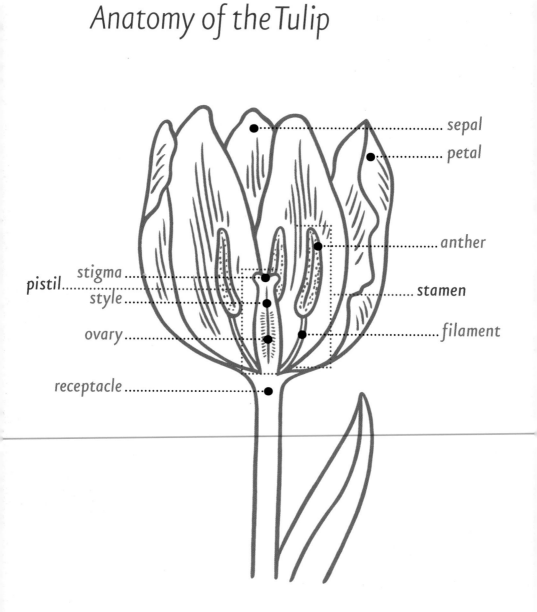

sepal

petal

anther

pistil

stigma

style

stamen

ovary

filament

receptacle

TULIPS ARE MEMBERS OF THE TULIPA GENUS, OF WHICH THERE ARE HUNDREDS OF SPECIES
AND THOUSANDS OF CULTIVARS (HYBRIDS). THEY RANGE IN SIZE FROM TINY JEWEL-LIKE
BLOSSOMS ON MIDGET PLANTS TO DARWIN HYBRIDS, WHICH ARE 2–3 FEET HIGH. TODAY TULIPS
ARE CULTIVATED AND ENJOYED ALL OVER THE WORLD. THE DUTCH—WITH MORE THAN
TWENTY-FOUR THOUSAND ACRES DEVOTED TO GROWING TULIPS—DOMINATE THE BULB
MARKET, AND THEIR BEST CUSTOMER IS THE UNITED STATES, FOLLOWED BY JAPAN, GERMANY,
FRANCE, AND ITALY. AMONG THE MOST POPULAR VARIETIES IS 'APRICOT BEAUTY,'
A SINGLE EARLY TULIP (OPPOSITE).

ILLUSTRATION: MEGAN MONTAGUE CASH

INTRODUCTION

TULIPS ARE among the world's best-known and most-beloved flowers. While roses rate as the number-one favorite, tulips have an undeniably great universal popularity and appeal. By investing a little time and a few dollars in tulip bulbs, you can fill your spring garden with a spectacular rainbow of colored blossoms. There are a great many varieties to choose from, with over three thousand currently in cultivation. And they are all beautiful.

Every year, in late winter, little nubs of tulip foliage emerge from the earth. Some are green, and some have wine-colored or cream stripes or mottling. While flower shapes do differ, most resemble the turbans after which they were named. They are available in every color imaginable except true blue and true black. Tulips can be tall or short, single or double; and they range from the bizarre Parrot to the classic flamboyant Rembrandt, from the green Viridiflora to the tiny Species and Kaufmanniana varieties. There is something for everyone and for every different kind of garden. In the United States, they are easily grown as far south as Zone 8, but can thrive in the South with special treatment. They are lovely in the garden and superb cut. Plant some. In fact, plant a lot. You won't regret it.

THIS PARROT TULIP 'SNOW PARROT' HAS NOT YET BEGUN TO SHOW OFF ITS FEATHER-LIKE PETALS. OVERLEAF: A SERPENTINE RIVER OF YELLOW EMPEROR TULIPS AND BLUE *MUSCARI* (GRAPE HYACINTHS) AT KEUKENHOF GARDENS, NEAR LISSE, HOLLAND. A SEVENTY-ACRE EXTRAVAGANZA, THIS HORTICULTURAL DISNEYLAND FEATURES MORE THAN SEVEN MILLION BULBS SET AMID HUNDREDS OF GLORIOUSLY FLOWERING TREES AND SHRUBS.

CLOCKWISE FROM UPPER LEFT: THE SPOTLIGHT IS ON THE LILY-SHAPED 'CHINA PINK' TULIPS WHILE THE BLEEDING HEART (*DICENTRA SPECTABILIS*) TAKES A BACKSEAT; THE EXTRAORDINARY COLORS OF DARWIN HYBRID TULIP 'OLYMPIC FLAME'; HOPE HENDLER'S NEW YORK CITY BACKYARD, A BEAUTIFUL SPRING BULB GARDEN; A MASTERPIECE OF BLUE *MUSCARI* FLANKED BY TULIPS AND DAFFODILS AT HOLLAND'S KEUKENHOF GARDENS.

1 *Tulips in History*

THE FIRST existing records we have of tulips derive from an ancient Persian legend. Far, far across the ocean, long, long ago, a handsome young prince named Farhad fell madly in love with a lovely young woman named Shirin. One day, Farhad received false word that his beloved had been killed. He was so griefstruck that he mounted his horse and galloped off a cliff to his death. It was said that a scarlet tulip grew and bloomed from the drops of his blood that had spilled on the earth. And so, in ancient Persia, the red tulip became a symbol of true love.

It is a widely held misconception that tulips are native to Holland, still growing wild in remote areas. Not so; in fact, almost no bulbous plants are native to that part of the world. From what we know, the first genetic center for tulips was in central Asia at a site in the Tien Shan and the Pamir Alai mountain ranges. From there, tulips spread east to China and Mongolia and also to the west and northwest. A secondary genetic center developed in Azerbaijan and Armenia and from there tulips spread to the Balkans, Spain, Portugal, Italy, Switzerland, and the south of France. Today about 150 tulip species are native to Europe.

But it was the Turks, during the days of the ancient Ottoman Empire, who first glorified the beauty of the tulip and began to grow and hybridize it. For them, tulips were a symbol of wealth and power, and the ancient sultans celebrated the flowers with lavish festivals that included colored lanterns, exotic birds in cages, and extravagant tulip arrangements. Tulips remain the national flower of Turkey to this day.

Tulips were never seen in Europe until 1554, until Austrian emperor Ferdinand I sent Ogier Ghiselin de Busbecque as his emissary to Constantinople to negotiate peace with Turkish Sultan Suleiman the Magnificent after the Turks' invasion of Hungary and siege of Vienna. De Busbecque's keen interest in botany led to the introduction of the tulip in Europe. While traveling from Adrianople (now Edirne) to

THIS DAINTY LITTLE GEM, SPECIES TULIP *T. TARDA*, IS NATIVE TO TURKESTAN. SPECIES TULIPS ARE IDEAL FOR USE IN ROCK GARDENS AND PERENNIALIZE EASILY.

Fosteriana, or Emperor, tulips at Filoli Gardens in California. The earliest of the medium-height tulips, their large flowers are like skyscrapers rising above a carpet of yellow.

Constantinople (now Istanbul), De Busbecque wrote that he saw "an abundance of flowers everywhere: narcissus, hyacinth, and those which the Turks called tulipam. Much to our astonishment because it was almost midwinter, a season unfriendly to flowers."

Although the Turkish word for tulip is *lale*, De Busbecque probably heard a description of the flower as looking like a *thoulypen* (the Turkish word for turban) and thought it was "tulipam," which ultimately was shortened to "tulip." He bought some bulbs, "which cost me not a little," according to his account. Upon returning to Vienna, he planted them in the imperial gardens, where they multiplied readily. Word of their existence and beauty spread.

Although representations of tulips, particularly those that today are called Lily-flowered, appeared in Turkish fabric design hundreds of years ago, the first accurate botanical drawing of a tulip did not appear in Europe until 1561. The Swiss botanist Konrad Gesner included one in a garden manual. Linnaeus, the renowned plant classifier, later named all garden tulips after him: *Tulipa gesneria*.

In 1593 Carolus Clusius, a Flemish botanist who had been imperial gardener in Vienna, went to Holland to chair the botany department at the University of Leiden. He brought with him a supply of tulips and planted them in his garden. Soon Clusius was besieged with extravagant offers for his prized specimens. According to one account, he decided to ask "such an exorbitant price that no one could procure them." But one night, while he slept, someone stole almost all the tulips from his garden. A period document relates that the thief "wasted no time in increasing them by sowing seeds, and by this means, the seventeen provinces of Holland were well stocked."

The romance of the tulip does not end here. New varieties of tulips occur when cultivated varieties "break," often unpredictably, producing new colors and markings. It was only recently that scientists have concluded that "breaks" are caused by a combination of natural mutations and a virus that spreads among the tulip bulbs. The result: flamboyantly striped and wildly colored tulips, which were highly prized by the rich of early seventeenth-century Europe.

In 1624, according to a contemporary report, one bulb of 'Semper Augustus,' a red-and-white tulip with a base of a blue tinge, sold at auction for $1,200. The next year the owner sold two propagated from the first for $3,000. Shortly three bulbs commanded $30,000. And so what has become known as tulipomania ensued, as all gardeners, rich and poor alike, realized that new varieties that might lead to untold riches could emerge from any bulb in any garden.

A decade later, the mania turned to madness, as bulb speculating tempted many. However what was being traded was not bulbs, but bulb futures, often bulbs that had not even bloomed yet. Men frantically mortgaged their houses and hocked the family jewels to raise money for tulip speculation. A brewer traded his brewery for one coveted bulb; a miller gave up his mill for another.

Then one spring day in 1637, the tulip market collapsed. Financial panic ensued. Fortunes were lost, with some investors even driven to suicide. The government banned further tulip speculation, and the Dutch turned to hybridizing and growing bulbs commercially as they do today.

As new varieties were introduced, word of their beauty spread. The striped tulips we call Rembrandts were popular with the Flemish and Dutch to the point that the great master painters of the era often included them in their canvases. The seventeenth-century French court favored fringed Parrot tulips. Through the eighteenth and nineteenth centuries, the Dutch were primarily involved with hybridizing and creating new varieties of tulips. The Darwin tulip, named for Charles Darwin, was bred in the late 1880s in Haarlem. At the time, experts claimed it was not new at all, but its sturdy stem and square-shaped base ultimately proved otherwise, and by 1892, the first Darwin tulip received the only gold medal at the Paris International Exhibition.

YOU CAN STILL plant some of the tulips that inspired tulipomania and graced the paintings of the Dutch old masters. Some of these varieties are exactly the same as their ancestors, and others are look-alikes that replicate historical varieties:

T. TARDA (dasystemon), 1590s. This multi-flowering Species tulip has chrome-yellow petals edged in bright white. The stunning, star-shaped blossoms open in mid-season. Topping the list of natural peren-nializers, *T. tarda* is 6 inches tall.

'KEIZERSKROON,' 1750. Boasting unusual red-edged-in-yellow flowers and a lovely scent, this old-time Single Early tulip has earned its place among the all-time great garden tulips. 13 inches tall.

Rembrandt tulips are rarely seen in American gardens. The petals are streaked, flushed, striped, feathered, splashed, and veined, often with contrasting colors. This one looks like it could have been painted by a Japanese artist.

Rembrandt tulips, 1610. These mottled (or "broken"-color) tulips launched the frenzy of trading that culminated in the near-collapse of the Dutch economy in 1637. There were many tulips in Dutch paintings of the era, but they were not a prominent theme in Rembrandt's own work—despite the fact that his name became attached to them.

T. clusiana, 1802. While the actual red-and-white-striped Species tulip *T. clusiana* is no longer commercially available, its new identical cousin is. The red-and-light-yellow striped *T. clusiana* 'Cynthia,' known also as the 'Peppermint' tulip, perennializes. 6 inches tall.

Viridiflora tulips, 1700. These stunning "green" tulips actually come in many colors, but their petals bear various sorts of green markings.

It appears that Dutch tulips and other flowering bulbs came to America via England and were first grown in the Philadelphia area. The American botanist John Bartram of Philadelphia, a colleague and friend of Benjamin Franklin and King George III's official botanist for North America, was perhaps the first to actually import the bulbs. Bartram, whose extensive correspondence with English botanist Peter Collinson has survived, received a supply of bulbs from Collinson in 1735. In 1739 Collinson sent some double tulips. In 1763 Bartram received "thousands of bulbs" from his English friend. Today, Bartram's house is preserved as a museum, and his Philadelphia garden—America's oldest surviving botanical garden, dating from 1728—is restored.

In 1750 William Logan, son of James Logan, who was William Penn's secretary, planted hyacinths and tulips imported from England in his garden at Stenton, Pennsylvania, and in 1770 Daniel Wister of Grublethorpe, Germantown, was growing "beds of tulips" and "named" hyacinths. Wister's beds seem to have been the first in America.

By the end of the century, tulips had become a primary planting on the great estates of America, as well as Europe. George Washington and Thomas Jefferson installed major plantings at Mount Vernon and Monticello. And tulips' popularity has never stopped growing.

T. clusiana 'Peppermint' tulip, *Anemone blanda*, and *Muscari* nestle under a tree, creating the feel of a woodland garden. Opposite above: Alfred Smith planted more than fifty varieties and close to three thousand tulips in his garden in Peconic, New York, creating one of the most impressive tulip plantings ever seen outside of a public or estate garden. Opposite below left: The pink of the bleeding heart echoes the colors of the Viridiflora tulip 'Greenland.' Opposite below right: The wonderful, whimsical Parrot tulip 'Green Wave.'

2 *Selecting Tulips*

IN 1996 the Royal General Bulbgrowers Association of the Netherlands divided the different species and cultivars of tulips into the following three classifications: early, mid-season, and late. For continuous tulip bloom each spring, select from all three categories. Within each there are different sizes—dwarf, medium, and tall—as well as differently shaped flowers. Consult this chapter carefully—the tulips are presented in the approximate order in which they bloom—and check the catalogues listed in the Source section, which usually have color photographs of the cultivars you will read about here. Then make your selection.

EARLY

SPECIES (BOTANICAL) TULIPS

Originally from the Mediterranean, Asia Minor, and the Caucasus, Species (or Botanical) tulips offer unusual flowers in varying heights and dazzling colors. Most are miniatures. If you haven't already discovered Species tulips, a wonderful world lies ahead. Different species bloom throughout the season, from early to late spring, but most are early spring bloomers and are especially prized for their jewel-like, bright colors: yellow, white, red, rose, purple, orange, or combinations thereof. The blossoms are 1–2 inches tall, in both water-lily and turban shapes, on erect 3–10-inch stems over medium-green foliage, some twisted. The bulbs are tiny, most the size of a nickel.

Be advised: Species tulips are so very charming that you might well become acquisitive and want more and more. Fear not, they are quite inexpensive and require little care and maintenance. The distinguished garden writer Louise Beebe Wilder wrote of Species tulips in her book *Adventures with Hardy Bulbs* in 1936 that "they open up to us a whole world of venture and adventure, they entice us to trial and experiment, calling

'PLAISIR,' A LOW-GROWING, EARLY-BLOOMING GREIGII TULIP, SPORTS WATER-LILY–SHAPED BLOOMS AND IS A PERFECT SELECTION FOR SPARKLING COLOR. IT IS EQUALLY LOVELY IN THE ROCK GARDEN OR INTERPLANTED AMONG FOUNDATION PLANTINGS.

us from the beaten track to little winding paths into the unknown."

Species tulips perennialize more readily than other tulips and are dazzling in rock gardens, either as sweet mini-clusters or naturalized in drifts. Do be aware, however, that burrowing creatures consider them gourmet treats during late winter. See Chapter 3 for further information.

Plant them in the fall, 3–4 inches deep, 3–4 inches apart in full or partial sun. Since they do perennialize naturally, before planting, fortify the soil with sphagnum peat moss and well-rotted compost or manure. Remove spent blossoms once tulips have bloomed, and remove foliage when it is withered and brown. Each spring, when shoots emerge, scratch in one tablespoon of 9-9-6 fertilizer per square foot of planting area. Give them space of their own, for they do not withstand competition from other plants, although they can cope with barren soils and severe weather.

Species tulips are a wonderful world that few are acquainted with. Plant a lot of them. You won't regret it.

ABOVE: *T. PRAESTANS* 'FUSILIER' WITH THE UNUSUAL *PUSCHKINIA SCILLOIDES*. OPPOSITE: WILD YELLOW TULIPS (LEFT) HAVE SLOWLY NATURALIZED OVER THE YEARS, TO OUR DELIGHT; *T. TARDA* LOOKS LOVELY IN FRONT OF ROCKS OR BOULDERS (RIGHT).

VARIETY	HEIGHT	DESCRIPTION
T. bakeri 'Lilac Wonder'	7"	Lilac and yellow
T. batalinii 'Apricot Jewel'	6"	Apricot-orange with yellow inside
T. batalinii 'Bright Gem'	6"	Sulfur-yellow–flushed warm orange
T. batalinii 'Red Jewel'	6"	Tiny; red
T. clusiana 'Lady Jane'	12"	Candy-cane rose and white
T. humilis	4"	Violet-pink with yellow base
T. humilis alba coerulea oculata	5"	White with blue base
T. kolpakowskiana	8"	Yellow-streaked red
T. linifolia	6"	Scarlet with black base
'Little Beauty'	4"	Cherry red with blue center
T. orphanidea flava	9"	Multi-flowering, yellow with red
T. praestans 'Fusilier'	8–12"	Multi-flowering; orange-scarlet
T. pulchella	4–6"	Pale purple

FOSTERIANA (EMPEROR) TULIPS

Fosteriana, or Emperor, tulips originated in Turkestan. They are the earliest of the medium-height tulips. Their flowers are remarkably large, and their colors are stunningly bright. They are exactly what gardeners want and need during the dreary late-winter and early-spring days, for they lift the spirits and offer forecasts of garden glories yet to come. Their show-stopping colors are often too bright for the late-spring garden, but earlier, they make welcome, dazzling displays when planted

LEFT: LAVENDER AND WHITE RHODODENDRONS ARE A COLORFUL BACKDROP FOR THE YELLOW-AND-WHITE FOSTERIANA 'SWEETHEART' TULIP. RIGHT: EMPEROR TULIPS COME IN AN ARRAY OF COLORS AND ARE EQUALLY EFFECTIVE IN FLOWER ARRANGEMENTS AND AS ACCENTS IN THE GARDEN.

in large drifts, and also serve well as cut flowers for indoor bouquets.

They are red, pink, yellow, white, orange, and combinations thereof. The 4-inch, turban-shaped blossoms are on 12–20-inch stems over medium-green or medium-green-and-purple broad-leafed foliage. They also tend to perennialize. I have a planting of classic red Emperors that is over ten years old. Each year it comes back, like an old friend visiting, to brighten my life. Until recently only solid colors were available, but each year, hybridizers offer new and interesting varieties, many of which are multicolored.

Plant them in the fall, 5–6 inches deep and 4–5 inches apart in full or partial sun. Remove spent blossoms once tulips have bloomed, and remove foliage when completely withered and brown. Since they do perennialize, fortify the soil with sphagnum peat moss and well-rotted compost or manure. They are good choices for naturalizing and are very lovely in woodland settings. Each spring, when shoots emerge, scratch in one tablespoon of 9-9-6 fertilizer per square foot of planting area. They bloom for about two weeks.

Here are some readily available varieties:

VARIETY	HEIGHT	DESCRIPTION
'Candela'	14"	Egg shaped; pure yellow
'Easter Parade'	16"	Carmine-rose and yellow
'Flaming Purissima'	18"	White brushed with rose
'Humoresque'	16"	Carmine-red with white edges
'Juan'	16"	Deep orange with yellow base
'Madame Lefeber' ('Red Emperor')	16"	Flaming red
'Orange Emperor'	16"	Soft orange, deep orange inside
'Princeps'	8"	Bright scarlet
'Purissima' ('White Emperor')	18"	White
'Rosy Dream'	14"	Rose with pale rose at edge
'Solva' ('Pink Emperor')	18"	Rose-flushed pale red
'Sweetheart'	16"	Lemon-yellow with white edge

TULIPS OF ALL SORTS LOOK WONDERFUL WITH OTHER SPRING FLOWERS, SUCH AS PANSIES AND CROCUSES. BY MAKING CAREFUL PLANTING CHOICES, YOU CAN GUARANTEE A COLORFUL DISPLAY ALL SPRING.

Kaufmanniana (Water-Lily) Tulips

Because of the shape of their blossoms, Kaufmanniana tulips are also known as Water-lily tulips. They are colorful, low-growing tulips perfect for rock gardens and border plantings. They have short stems and large flowers with slightly reflexed petals. They hug the ground and are wind resistant; some varieties have beautiful mottled foliage. All open fully on sunny days to reveal multi-colored interiors. They may naturalize for years when left undisturbed in a spot where they are happy. They bloom in early spring, after the first of the Species tulips.

They are salmon, scarlet, yellow, cream, apricot, orange, and combinations thereof. Their blossoms are on 6–12-inch stems over medium-green and burgundy or medium-green and white foliage.

Plant them in the fall 5–6 inches deep and 3–6 inches apart in full or partial sun. Remove spent blossoms once tulips have bloomed. Remove foliage when completely withered and brown. They do perennialize, so be sure to fortify the soil with sphagnum peat moss and well-rotted compost or manure. Each spring, when shoots emerge, scratch in one tablespoon of 9-9-6 fertilizer per square foot of planting area. They bloom for about two weeks. Be sure to provide rodent protection.

VARIETY	HEIGHT	DESCRIPTION
'Ancilla'	6"	Pink and white
'Chopin'	6"	Lemon yellow
'Fritz Kriesler'	6"	Salmon-pink
'Gaiety'	8"	Rose-violet edged in cream
'Gold Coin'	6–8"	Scarlet edged with yellow
'Heart's Delight'	10"	Carmine and rose
'Shakespeare'	6–8"	Salmon-orange-apricot
'Showwinner'	6–8"	Scarlet
'Stresa'	7"	Gold with orange border
'Vivaldi'	7"	Yellow and crimson
'Waterlily'	7"	Cream and carmine

SINGLE EARLY TULIPS

These glimmering cup-shaped tulips bloom long before any of their long-stemmed siblings but later than the Emperor tulips. They reach a height of 12–16 inches. Since their stems are quite strong, they withstand early spring winds and rain, opening fully only in sunny weather. The flowers are long lasting—they bloom for about three weeks—because early spring temperatures are cool. Many are fragrant, and they are excellent for bedding and forcing.

They are available in all colors of the rainbow. The 5-inch, turban-shaped blossoms grow over medium-green, broad-leafed foliage. Plant them in the fall, 5 inches deep and 5–6 inches apart in full sun or partial shade. Remove spent blossoms once tulips have bloomed, and remove foliage when it is completely withered and brown.

VARIETY	HEIGHT	DESCRIPTION
'Beauty Queen'	16"	Apricot-salmon with pale yellow
'Bellona'	14"	Golden yellow and fragrant
'Bestseller'	16"	Bright salmon
'Christmas Dream'	12"	Carmine-rose with white base
'Christmas Marvel'	12"	Cherry-pink; fragrant
'Color Cardinal'	12"	Scarlet-red–flushed plum
'Flair'	14"	Bright-yellow–flamed raspberry
'General de Wet'	13"	Orange; very fragrant
'Princess Irene'	12"	Orange with purple; very fragrant
'Purple Prince'	14"	Lilac-purple
'White Cascade'	12"	Pure white

'CHRISTMAS DREAM,' A LOVELY SINGLE EARLY TULIP. SINGLE EARLY TULIPS ARE STURDY AND LONG LASTING, AND ARE PERFECT FOR BEDS, BORDERS, AND FORCING INDOORS.

DOUBLE EARLY TULIPS

Cousins of the Single Early tulips, these semi-double- to double-flowered cultivars are short stemmed, early flowering, and long lasting. They can withstand temperature changes and the heavy wind and rains of early spring, and have peony- and rose-like bloom. Many varieties are excellent for forcing and are quite fragrant.

Like the Single Early tulips, they are available in all colors of the rainbow. The 5-inch, peony-shaped blossoms are on 10–12-inch stems over medium-green, broad-leafed foliage. Because they are short, some are appropriate for dooryard gardens or rock gardens. Plant them in the fall, 5 inches deep and 5–6 inches apart in full or partial sun. Remove spent blossoms once tulips have bloomed—they bloom for about three weeks—and remove the foliage only when it is completely withered and brown.

VARIETY	HEIGHT	DESCRIPTION
'Abba'	10"	Bright tomato-red; fragrant
'Electra'	10"	Cherry
'Monsella'	10"	Bright yellow, feathered red, fragrant
'Monte Carlo'	10"	Yellow; fragrant
'Montreux'	10"	Ivory-yellow with rose blush; fragrant
'Peach Blossom'	12"	Rose-pink
'Schoonoord'	10"	Pure white; fragrant
'Sven Dahlman'	10"	Cherry-pink with purple

IN APRIL CANDYTUFT (*IBERIS*) CONTRASTS BEAUTIFULLY WITH EARLY TULIPS AND HYACINTHS AT THE EDGE OF THE BORDER.

Greigii Tulips

These tulips grow to 10–14 inches tall and follow the Kaufmanniana bloom in early spring. Like the Kaufmannianas, the blossoms resemble water lilies and the color combinations are dazzling, but the flowers are slightly larger. The foliage is particularly interesting, with mottled and streaked stripes of maroon, brown, or deep purple. Their short stature makes them ideal for the front of the border and for rock gardens.

They are orange, red, yellow, gold, cream, pink, ivory, and combinations thereof. The blossoms are on stems 6–20 inches over the mottled foliage. They tend to perennialize. I have seen plantings of the bright 'Red Riding Hood,' the best known of this group, bloom in a nearby garden for the past twenty-five years. Provide rodent protection if you want them to perennialize.

Plant them in the fall, 6 inches deep, 3–6 inches apart in full or partial sun. Remove spent blossoms once tulips have bloomed, and remove foliage when completely withered and brown. Since they do perennialize, before planting, fortify the soil with sphagnum peat moss and well-rotted compost or manure. Each spring, when shoots emerge, scratch in one tablespoon of 9-9-6 fertilizer per square foot of planting area. They bloom for about three weeks.

VARIETY	HEIGHT	DESCRIPTION
'Calypso'	12"	Red with yellow edges
'Cape Cod'	12–14"	Orange-red, yellow inside
'Corsage'	10–12"	Rose-feathered yellow
'Czar Peter'	10"	White feathered with rose
'Donna Bella'	12"	Carmine red with cream edges
'Elise'	12"	Cream-yellow with coral pink
'Engadin'	12"	Yellow edged with deep red
'Lovely Surprise'	18"	Rich red
'Mary Ann'	14"	Carmine red edged with white
'Oratorio'	10"	Rose pink
'Oriental Splendour'	20"	Lemon edged with carmine-red
'Pinocchio'	10"	Red with white edges
'Plaisir'	12"	Cream edged with carmine red
'Red Riding Hood'	6–8"	Brilliant scarlet
'Royal Splendour'	20"	Scarlet
'Scheherazade'	12"	Scarlet
'Sweet Lady'	8"	Soft pink and ivory
'Toronto'	14"	Multi-flowered; tangerine red
'United States'	14"	Orange-flamed scarlet

GREIGII TULIP 'PLAISIR' (LEFT) IS EFFECTIVE WITH EARLY-BLOOMING MINOR BULBS SUCH AS *CHIONODOXA* AND *SCILLA*. RIGHT: 'RED RIDING HOOD' LOOKS STUNNING INTERPLANTED WITH DUTCH CROCUSES.

MID-SEASON

DARWIN HYBRID TULIPS

Giant Darwin Hybrids were introduced to the United States by John
Scheepers, Inc., as recently as 1951. Their flowers are the largest of all
tulips, and they grow taller than almost all others. They were bred by
crossing the lovely colorful varieties of Darwin tulips with the early
blooming, weather-resistant Fosteriana (Emperor) tulips. Flowering
from mid-April to early May, these stately tulips are excellent for spectacular garden displays, bedding, and flower arrangements.

They are red, yellow, pink, white, orange, purple, and combinations
thereof. The large turban-shaped blossoms are on 22–30-inch stems over
medium green, broad-leafed foliage. They perennialize quite well, as
long as they are fed annually and are in a sunny spot with well-drained
soil. I have some plantings that are more than ten years old. In fact,
there is one 'Golden Apeldoorn' that dates back twenty years and is in
the wrong place in the garden. Despite the fact that this single yellow
tulip looks slightly ridiculous where it is, I have decided to leave it there,
out of respect for its determination. Because of their tough nature and
the fact that many varieties do perennialize, Darwin Hybrid tulips have
become extremely popular and every year hybridizers introduce more
and more varieties.

Plant them in the fall, 6 inches deep and about 6 inches apart in full
sun or partial shade. They are available in all colors of the rainbow. The
5-inch, turban-shaped blossoms are on 12–16-inch stems over medium-
green, broad-leafed foliage. Remove spent blossoms once tulips have
bloomed, and remove foliage when complete withered and brown. They
bloom for about three weeks. Each spring, when shoots emerge, scratch
in one tablespoon of 9-9-6 fertilizer per square foot of planting area.
They bloom at about the time when early-blooming tulips such as Greigii,
Emperor, and Kaufmannianas are ending their bloom cycle. If you are
planning a display to bloom in conjunction with azaleas and dogwoods,
these are just a bit too early. Select from the late-blooming tulips instead.

STATELY DARWIN HYBRID TULIPS ARE TALL ENOUGH TO BE NOTICED AGAINST THE BACK FENCE
OF OUR PROPERTY. WITH THE LARGEST BLOOMS OF ALL TULIPS, THESE GOOD PERENNIALIZERS
COME IN A WIDE ARRAY OF COLORS.

VARIETY	HEIGHT	DESCRIPTION
'Apeldoorn'	23"	Brilliant red
'Big Chief'	24"	Rose-salmon with yellow base
'Cream Jewel'	24"	Ivory white
'Daydream'	22"	Apricot orange
'Fringed Elegance'	24"	Fringed primrose yellow
'Golden Apeldoorn'	24"	Gold-yellow
'Ivory Floradale'	22"	Pure white
'Ollioules'	22"	Rose-red with ivory white
'Pink Impression'	22"	Clear pink
'Tender Beauty'	22"	Rose-red and creamy white

Triumph Tulips

Another mid-spring variety is the Triumph. They bloom when the early tulips are just about finished, and about two weeks before the late-blooming tulips. For this reason, they are very popular. They are a cross between the Mayflowering Darwin and Single Early tulips, and sport large, shapely blooms on good strong stems. They thrive in drastic changes of temperature and resist heavy wind and rain.

They are available in almost every color of the rainbow. The large, turban-shaped blossoms are on 16–26-inch stems over medium-green foliage. Some varieties do perennialize.

Triumph tulips 'Shirley' and 'Negrita' bloom at the same time as daffodils in this Long Island garden. The charming sculpture of an angel completes the picture.

Plant them in the fall, 5–6 inches deep and 5 inches apart in full or partial sun. Remove spent blossoms once tulips have bloomed, and remove foliage when completely withered and brown. Triumphs bloom for about three weeks. Since some varieties do perennialize, fortify soil with sphagnum peat moss and well-rotted compost or manure before planting. Each spring, when varieties that perennialize send up their shoots, scratch in one tablespoon of 9-9-6 fertilizer per square foot of planting area.

There are a great many varieties of Triumphs available, and hybridizers introduce new ones every year. This is because they are the most popular tulip for professional forcing. Most of the tulips you see in pots around Easter are Triumphs. They offer a fine display the first year, but rarely perennialize.

VARIETY	HEIGHT	DESCRIPTION
'Anna Jose'	20"	Rose
'Annie Schilder'	18"	Warm orange; very fragrant
'Barcelona'	20"	Hot fuchsia
'Bastogne'	18"	Deep red
'Calgary'	8–10"	Ivory-white–flamed cream-yellow
'Cream Perfection'	18"	Cream-yellow
'Dreaming Maid'	20"	Pink with white edges
'Glowing Pink'	20"	Rose with darker flames and pink edges
'Golden Melody'	20"	Buttercup yellow
'Hans Anrud'	22"	Purple
'Jo-Ann'	20"	Soft pink with white base
'Leen van der Mark'	20"	Cardinal red with yellow edges
'Palestrina'	16"	Salmon-pink with green feathering
'Passionale'	16"	Deep purple

A LOVELY ARRAY OF LILY-FLOWERING TULIPS (CLOCKWISE FROM TOP LEFT): 'WEST POINT,'
FLOURISHING IN A ROCK GARDEN; 'WHITE TRIUMPHATOR' AT THE EDGE OF A POND; 'MONA LISA,'
A STANDOUT IN ANY GARDEN; AND 'BALLADE,' GLOWING WITH A SPECIAL LIGHT.

LATE

Lily-Flowered Tulips

Elegant Lily-flowered tulips became very popular during the days of the Sultans in Turkey to the degree that they became a widespread motif in Turkish design. During the late sixteenth century these tulips were imported into Europe, but as the years went by, Europeans preferred the cup- or egg-shaped varieties. But today the Lily-flowered tulip is once again very popular.

The petals of this tulip are reflexed and curved atop strong tall stems. The colors are subdued yet warm, and the cup-shaped blossoms have gently pointed tips. They are long lasting when cut and bloom in the garden for about three weeks.

Plant them in the fall, 5–6 inches deep and 4–5 inches apart in full or partial sun. Remove spent blossoms once tulips have bloomed, and remove foliage when completely withered and brown.

VARIETY	HEIGHT	DESCRIPTION
'Ballade'	22"	Reddish magenta, white edges
'Ballerina'	22"	Lemon with scarlet flames
'China Pink'	18"	Soft pink with white base
'Cistula'	22"	Lemon with pale-yellow base
'Elegant Lady'	20"	Pale cream-yellow, violet edges
'Mariette'	22"	Rose with white base.
'Marilyn'	22"	Candy-cane red and white
'Mona Lisa'	22"	Yellow with raspberry flames
'Queen of Sheba'	24"	Mahogany red with gold tips
'Red Shine'	22"	Deep red
'West Point'	20"	Primrose yellow
'White Triumphator'	24"	Pure white
'Yonina'	16"	Cherry

Multi-Flowered (Bouquet) Tulips

The Multi-flowered, or Bouquet, tulip is another class of tulip rarely seen in American gardens. Each tulip bulb produces a bouquet of at least four to six full-sized flowers per stem, creating a garden display that is nothing short of sensational. The brilliantly colored large flowers are cup shaped in white, yellow-flamed red, pink, red-orange, scarlet, ivory, violet candy cane, and fringed violet pink. The large blooms are on 14–20-inch stems over medium green foliage.

Plant them in the fall, 5–6 inches deep and 4–5 inches apart in full sun or partial shade. Remove spent blossoms once tulips have bloomed, and remove foliage when completely withered and brown. They are not reliable perennializers, so to assure a display every year, dig them after bloom, and plant new ones each fall. They bloom for about two weeks.

VARIETY	HEIGHT	DESCRIPTION
'Bridal Bouquet'	18"	Pure white
'Candy Club'	18"	Ivory white with pale violet feathering
'Color Spectacle'	20"	Canary yellow with cardinal flames
'Fringed Family'	22"	Violet-pink with lighter edges
'Georgette'	20"	Clear yellow with scarlet edge
'Happy Family'	20"	Rose-pink
'Modern Style'	20"	Ivory white brushed with pale purple
'Orange Bouquet'	20"	Red-orange
'Red Bouquet'	20"	Clear scarlet with yellow base
'Toronto'	14"	Pink-tinged red foliage
'White Bouquet'	20"	Pure white

PARROT TULIPS

These exotic tulips, with their flamboyantly fringed and scalloped petals and sensational striations, are great favorites of decorators and landscape designers alike. They are bound to stop traffic in any garden, and are sure to be a conversation piece.

Late-blooming tulips with very large flowers, Parrots are available in a wide range of colors. Their petals open wide and lie flat on the 16–20-inch stems. Some feel they are garish; however, if used in moderation, they provide startling focal points in any garden.

Plant them in the fall, 5–6 inches deep and 4–5 inches apart in full sun or partial shade. Remove spent blossoms once tulips have bloomed, and remove foliage when completely withered and brown. Parrot tulips are not reliable perennially, so if you want to be sure of a display, dig tulips after they bloom and plant new ones in the fall.

VARIETY	HEIGHT	DESCRIPTION
'Apricot Parrot'	20"	Apricot with cream-white; fragrant
'Black Parrot'	20"	Purple-black and fringed
'Blue Parrot'	22"	Bright violet with bluish-bronze tinge
'Estella Rynveld'	22"	Red with white flames
'Fantasy'	22"	Salmon-pink feathered with green stripes
'Flaming Parrot'	22"	Bright yellow flamed with red
'Green Wave'	20"	Pastel mauve pink with green flames
'Orange Favorite'	20"	Deep orange with green markings
'Texas Gold'	18"	Deep yellow with red edge
'White Parrot'	18"	Pure white with green

48

Peony (Double Late) Tulips

Because of the shape and size of these multi-petaled blossoms and their similarity to peony blooms, these Double Late tulips are often called Peony-flowered tulips. The most popular variety is 'Angelique,' a lovely pale pink with lighter and darker pink accents on the edges. It is enticingly fragrant.

Peony tulips are pink, deep maroon, blue, yellow, lilac, white, orange, and wine red. The blowsy blossoms are on 12–20-inch stems over medium-green, broad-leafed foliage. Perennialization is not reliable; I do have a planting of 'Angelique' tulips that comes up each spring, but it is depleting with each year. For reliable bloom, dig up bulbs after they bloom, and plant new ones every fall. They bloom for about two weeks.

VARIETY	HEIGHT	DESCRIPTION
'Angelique'	18"	Pale pink with darker pink flushes
'Carnaval de Nice'	20"	White, feathered and flamed red
'Creme Upstar'	14"	Primrose-yellow with green and magenta
'Gold Medal'	16"	Deep yellow
'Hermione'	20"	Violet-rose with white
'Maravilla'	20"	Violet; fragrant
'Maywonder'	20"	Deep rose; fragrant
'Miranda'	22"	Red with lemon base; fragrant
'Mount Tacoma'	20"	Pure white with green marks; fragrant
'Upstar'	18"	Creamy white to rose-pink; fragrant

Bizarre and flamboyant, Parrot tulips are fun! Their contorted shapes are forever changing as they reach their full bloom. Planted in moderation, they provide focal points and conversation pieces in any garden.

Rembrandt Tulips

This group of flamboyantly baroque tulips is another rarely seen in American gardens. They are sometimes referred to as "broken" tulips. The petals have streaked, flushed, striped, feathered, splashed, veined, and often contrasting colors. You often see these flowers in the paintings of the Flemish and Dutch masters. They are one of the few classes of tulips that are attractive when planted as mixtures in a landscape. The restoration of the Het Loo Palace gardens in Apeldoorn, Holland, includes many of these wonderfully weird tulips.

Plant them in the fall, 5–6 inches deep and 4–5 inches apart in full or partial sun. Remove spent blossoms once tulips have bloomed, and remove foliage when completely withered and brown. Since they often perennialize, fortify the soil with sphagnum peat moss and well-rotted compost or manure before planting. Since they naturalize, they are very lovely in woodland settings. Each spring, when shoots emerge, scratch in one tablespoon of 9-9-6 fertilizer per square foot of planting area. They bloom for about two weeks. Rembrandt tulips are usually sold in mixtures, but individual varieties are also available.

VARIETY	HEIGHT	DESCRIPTION
'Black Boy'	20"	Mahogany with clear-yellow feathering
'Cordell Hull'	24"	Red and white
'Madame Dubarry'	20"	Yellow with apricot blotches
'Zomerschoon'	20"	Red with white

The blue of the *Muscari* (grape hyacinth) complements the pale 'Angelique' Peony tulip grown in our woodland garden. 'Angelique' has been one of the most popular tulips in America for years.

FRINGED (CRISPA) TULIPS

Another tulip variety rarely seen in American gardens, the Fringed tulip is also known as the Crispa tulip. The petals of these cup-shaped blossoms are edged with crystal-shaped fringes, unlike any other tulips. Some call them "tulips to touch" because most people can't resist testing the flower's fringe to see if it is real or glass. They are available in a wide range of colors and are tall, 18–26 inches.

Plant them in the fall, 5–6 inches deep and 4–5 inches apart in full sun or partial shade. Remove spent blossoms once tulips have bloomed. Remove foliage when completely withered and brown. Since they perennialize, before planting fortify the soil with sphagnum peat moss and well-rotted compost or manure. They are very lovely in woodland settings, since they naturalize. Each spring, when shoots emerge, scratch in one tablespoon of 9-9-6 fertilizer per square foot of planting area. They bloom for about two weeks.

VARIETY	HEIGHT	DESCRIPTION
'Aleppo'	20"	Raspberry-rose with apricot
'Bellflower'	24"	Rose with blue-white base
'Burgundy Lace'	26"	Wine-red with crystalline fringed edge
'Canova'	24"	Cobalt-violet tinted purple
'Fancy Frills'	18"	Ivory white blending to rose pink
'Fringed Elegance'	24"	Yellow with pale crystalline fringe
'Fringed Family'	18"	Violet-rose with ivory base
'Lambada'	20"	Rose-salmon with yellow edge
'Swan Wings'	22"	Pure white with fringed edge

PEOPLE CAN'T RESIST TOUCHING 'CANOVA,' A FRINGED TULIP, WHICH BLOOMS FOR ABOUT TWO WEEKS. OVERLEAF: A SPRING GARDEN FEATURING DARWIN HYBRID TULIPS AND THE UNUSUAL *FRITILLARIA PERSICA,* AMONG OTHERS.

Viridiflora (Green) Tulips

Very rarely seen in American gardens, Viridiflora tulips are among my favorite spring plants. All varieties have prominent green markings and feathering on the petals. They are long lasting both in a vase and in the garden and certainly add an exotic touch to any landscape.

As with all varieties of tulips, plant them in the fall, 5–6 inches deep and 4–5 inches apart in full or partial sun. Remove spent blossoms once tulips have bloomed, and remove foliage when completely withered and brown. They may perennialize for a few years, but for certain bloom, remove spent tulips and replant every year.

VARIETY	HEIGHT	DESCRIPTION
'Artist'	14–16"	Salmon-rose with green markings
'Formosa'	12"	Yellow and green
'Golden Artist'	14–16"	Gold-yellow with pink and green feathering
'Greenland'	20"	Old rose with green stripes
'Hollywood Star'	12"	Green-flamed brilliant red
'Pimpernel'	16"	Pure red with green feathering
'Spring Green'	20"	Ivory-white with soft-green feathering
'Violet Queen'	20"	Violet-purple brushed green

Single Late (Mayflowering) Tulips

Darwin tulips, named after Charles Darwin, were hybridized during the late nineteenth century. Cottage tulips were popular in the cottage gardens of England as long ago as the eighteenth century, and have sustained their popularity. Several years ago, the two classes merged to become "Single Late" or "Mayflowering" tulips because, as a result of hybridization, the differences between them are no longer noticeable. They are the most popular group of all the tulips, due to their consistent, reliable performance for both cutting and mass plantings. Blooms are large, with classic tulip shape, borne on long, strong stems up to 30 inches tall, and are available in an enormous range of colors, many solid-colored.

Plant them in the fall, 6–8 inches deep and 5–6 inches apart in full or partial sun. Remove spent blossoms once tulips have bloomed, and remove foliage when completely withered and brown. Mayflowering tulips are not reliable perennializers, but I have a number of plantings that are more than five years old and still put on a display every spring. In most parts of the country, Mayflowering tulips bloom at the same time as dogwood, azaleas, and some rhododendrons, and just before irises, peonies, and lilacs. Keep this in mind when you design your spring landscape.

VARIETY	HEIGHT	DESCRIPTION
'Big Smile'	26"	Lemon yellow
'Dillenburg'	24"	Burnt-orange terra-cotta; sweet fragrance
'Dordogne'	26"	Claret-rose
'Duke of Wellington'	26"	Pure white
'Kingsblood'	24"	Dark cherry-red
'Maureen'	28"	Marble-white
'Menton'	26"	Rose pink
'Mrs. John T. Scheepers'	26"	Golden yellow
'Queen of Bartignons'	22"	Salmon-pink with white base
'Queen of Night'	24"	Known as the Black Tulip
'Sweet Harmony'	24"	Lemon-yellow–edged white

FRAGRANT TULIPS

If you plan on cutting tulips for indoor arrangements, you might wish to consider varieties that have more fragrance than others. The most fragrant of all tulips are:

VARIETY	COLOR	BLOOM TIME
'Ad Rem' (Darwin Hybrid)	Red-orange	Mid-season
'Angelique' (Double Late)	Blush pink with white	Late
'Apricot Parrot' (Parrot)	Apricot, pink, green	Late
'Ballerina' (Lily-flowered)	Marigold orange	Late
'Christmas Marvel' (Single Early)	Cherry-pink	Early
'Dillenburg' (Single Late)	Orange, terra cotta	Late
'Keizerskroon' (Single Early)	Red-edged yellow	Early
'Mr. van der Hoef' (Double Early)	Yellow	Early
'Princess Irene' (Triumph)	Orange-flamed purple	Mid-season
T. tarda (Species)	Yellow, edged white	Mid-season

OPPOSITE: A CONSIDERABLE DISPLAY OF SPECIES TULIP T. *TARDA* IN A ROCK GARDEN. ALWAYS TRY TO PLANT AS MANY OF THESE SMALL BULBS AS POSSIBLE FOR AN OVER-THE-TOP EFFECT. ABOVE: THESE EYE-CATCHING MAYFLOWERING TULIPS HAVE OPENED THEIR PETALS WIDE TO TAKE IN SOME SUN. THEY WILL FOLD UP TO PROVIDE A MORE RESPECTABLE SHOW AS THE AFTERNOON MOVES ON.

3 Growing Tulips

YOU'VE PROBABLY noticed the enormous banners advertising Dutch bulbs that appear at garden centers, nurseries, and even supermarkets toward the end of summer and the beginning of fall. Fall is the time to buy and plant tulips and other bulbs. But don't limit your tulip bulb buying to what is available at these local sources. Mail-order nurseries (see Sources, page 95) offer a wider selection. Simply request their free catalogues in June or July, and place your order by the beginning of August to be assured of getting what you want. Almost all mail-order companies deliver bulbs at the proper planting time for your area.

GETTING STARTED

Tulips need time in order to bloom. After they are planted, they don't just sit there underground waiting for spring; they soon push small roots from their base, and then, a little later, stems from their pointed tops. The stems reach upward, often to within less than an inch of the surface of the soil. Then they stop, even if winter has not yet set in. Sometimes, during a late-winter thaw, the stems pop up above the surface of the soil, but when the cold returns, they stop growing again. This does not harm the bulbs. With the warm weather and sun of spring, they grow again—this time until they bloom.

Tulips require a chilling period in the ground in order to bloom. In general, tulips thrive in areas in which the temperature goes down to 20°F in the winter. But there are five Species tulips that don't need a cold period to flower and will naturalize faithfully in Southern states: *T. clusiana* 'Cynthia', *T. clusiana* 'Candy Tulip,' *T. saxatilis*, *T. sylvestris*, *T. clusiana chrysantha*, and *T. bakeri* 'Lilac Wonder.'

Other tulips may be grown in warm climates but should be treated

A PERFECT LIVING ARRANGEMENT: THE YELLOW SMEAR ON THE RED LILY-FLOWERING TULIPS 'QUEEN OF SHEBA' IS REPEATED IN THE YELLOW MAYFLOWERING TULIPS AND OFFSET BY THE DEEP BLUE OF THE *MUSCARI* (GRAPE HYACINTH). OVERLEAF: KEEP YOUR COLOR SCHEME SIMPLE. HERE, YELLOW PREDOMINATES, WITH PEONIES, DAFFODILS, AND DARWIN HYBRID TULIPS STATING THE THEME. ONE SPLASH OF PINK PROVIDED BY THE AZALEA COMPLETES THE COMPOSITION.

as annuals—expect to dig them up after they bloom in the spring, and plant more in the fall—and given some special care. The trick is to give them a "cold treatment" for eight to ten weeks. You can do this by storing them in vented paper bags in a refrigerator. First remove any fruit in the refrigerator, as the ethylene gas given off by ripening fruit will kill the flower embryos inside the bulbs. Take the bulbs directly from the refrigerator to the planting site in November or early December. When choosing a site avoid southern exposures and plant in areas that get morning sun or partial shade so that your flowers will last longer. Plant 6–8 inches deep with a 2-inch layer of mulch.

SELECTING A SITE

The first thing to consider when choosing a site is light. Tulips require either full or partial sun in order to perform well.

Then consider drainage. Tulips require good drainage to grow properly. Beyond the obvious—to avoid swampy soil or areas where water gathers after rain—you can test a site by digging a hole the depth at which the bulb will be planted. Fill it with water and allow it to soak in. Repeat this two times. If it takes more than six hours for the water to soak in the last time, the drainage in this location is not sufficient, and you should select another site.

PREPARING THE SOIL

Once you have selected the site, you must prepare the soil. If the soil lacks organic matter, and thus nutrients for the plants, success in growing tulips will be quite limited. While soil fortification does require some work, it will definitely help ensure good long-term results.

To prepare the soil, excavate the planting area to a depth of at least one foot, placing the soil on top of a drop cloth as you dig. This will help keep the surrounding area tidy and make the job of replacing the soil easier. Remove and dispose of stones and other debris. Then mix the excavated soil with organic material in a ratio of two parts soil to one part organic material. You can use sphagnum peat moss, well-rotted manure, compost, or a combination of all three. Shovel the mixture into the excavated bed, and water thoroughly. It is best to do this several days in advance of your tulip planting.

PLANTING AND FERTILIZING TULIPS

Once you have designed your garden, purchased the bulbs, selected the site, and fortified the bed, it is time to plant. Bring a ruler so you can measure the depth and spacing of the bulbs. Be sure you have your design scheme as well. And, don't worry if the brown paper coverings, called tunics, come off the bulbs. This won't do any harm.

As a general rule, you should dig a hole that is twice as deep as the recommended depth for a particular tulip bulb. Replace the soil to the recommended planting level and flatten it by patting the bottom gently with your hand. This will ensure an even surface for the bulbs so they won't fall over when you refill the hole. Set the bulbs in place with their pointed ends up and gently press them into the soil. Cover the bulbs with the rest of the soil, tamp down lightly, and water thoroughly. If there are dry spells in your area during the fall or spring, water your planting thoroughly at least once a week.

Depending on your plans, you may need some fertilizer. Once upon a time, bone meal was considered an excellent bulb fertilizer, but times have changed! Today, most bone meal is so thoroughly processed that most of the essential nutrients have literally been boiled out. On top of that, dogs and other critters can sniff it out and will be tempted to dig. If you're planting tulips for only one year's bloom, fertilizer is not needed. A healthy Dutch bulb will already contain a season's supply of food in the moist tissue surrounding the embryonic flower. If you want your tulips to perennialize, however, that's a different matter.

PERENNIALIZING TULIPS

In Holland, and indeed throughout Europe, most gardeners treat tulips as annuals. That is, they plant them in the fall, enjoy them in the spring, and then dig them up and throw them away. They do this because they know that most tulips produce less and less bloom with each passing year. Here in America, however, we tend to think in terms of permanent perennial plantings, so we plant tulips and then several years down the line wonder why they no longer produce spectacular bloom. The reason is that tulip bulbs divide into small bulbs each year, and if the planting is not fertilized and the soil and climate are not ideal, they deplete.

Still, the fact is that tulips actually are true perennials. "Getting them to bloom in your garden year after year is no problem," says Frans Roozen, technical director of the International Flower Bulb Center in Hillegom, the Netherlands. "As long as your garden happens to be located in the foothills of the Himalayas, or the steppes of eastern Turkey." The tulip is at its perennial best in conditions that match the cold winters and hot, dry summers of its native regions.

To get the bulbs to not only perennialize, but to multiply, is a bit more problematic. "The growers in Holland subject their plant stock to a series of heat and humidity treatments each summer before planting," explains Roozen. By the time the bulbs are tucked into the sandy Dutch soil for their winter's sleep and "cold treatment," they have been fooled into thinking they've been through another summer drought in the Himalayas. You cannot do this at home in this country.

Thus, most tulips cannot be counted on to enhance your garden after a year or two. Some varieties are more prone to perennialize than others, but they must be fertilized properly to achieve this effect.

These include the Species tulips, which are the earliest to bloom and the closest genetically to the original wild tulips. If a particular variety is prone to perennialize, the description on the package or in the catalogue will probably say "for naturalizing," or something to that effect. Also, many of the Kaufmanniana, Fosteriana (Emperor), and Griegii do perennialize and multiply, providing beautiful displays year after year. The spectacular Darwin Hybrids also tend to perennialize if conditions are favorable.

If you wish to try to perennialize recommended varieties of tulips, you should provide one of the three following feeding options when you plant the bulbs:

1. Work a good organic compost or well-rotted cow manure into the soil, and add a mulch of this material on top.

2. Work in a slow-release bulb food (9-9-6) at the rate of one table-spoon per square foot.

3. Work in a fast-release soluble fertilizer (8-8-8 or 10-10-10) at the rate of one tablespoon per square foot.

In the spring, no fertilizer is needed for first-year blooms. For naturalized plantings or perennializing plants, nothing further is needed if you applied well-rotted cow manure in the fall. If you used a slow-release bulb food or a fast-release fertilizer, apply a nitrogen-rich fast-release fertilizer in the spring just as the shoots first emerge from the soil (about six weeks prior to bloom).

The Netherlands bulb industry in connection with the North Carolina State University Arboretum has run trial plantings of specific varieties of Dutch tulips for four years to test their tendency to perennialize. The varieties that performed best are listed below. The trials run by North Carolina State University were planted in zones 7, 8, and 9, among the milder climatic regions of the country. This does not necessarily mean that these tulip varieties will not do as well in cooler zones, and similar results in your garden, no matter where it is, are not guaranteed.

Almost all Species tulips and Darwin Hybrids in yellow, red, orange, and combinations thereof tend to perennialize. Among the best early and mid-season performers are:

SPECIES TULIP 'LITTLE PRINCESS' WILL MULTIPLY READILY, ADDING COLOR IN FRONT OF A BORDER OR IN A ROCK GARDEN.

VARIETY	CLASSIFICATION	DESCRIPTION
'Ad Rem'	Darwin Hybrid	Yellow edged with red
'Apeldoorn's Elite'	Darwin Hybrid	Red with orange-yellow
'Beauty of Apeldoorn'	Darwin Hybrid	Orange-yellow and red striped
'Charles'	Single Early	Deep red
'Couleur Cardinal'	Single Early	Violet-red
'Golden Apeldoorn'	Darwin Hybrid	Yellow
'Golden Parade'	Darwin Hybrid	Yellow
'Gudoshnik'	Darwin Hybrid	Orange fringed with yellow
'Jewel of Spring'	Darwin Hybrid	Red edged with yellow
'Monte Carlo'	Double Early	Yellow
'Negrita'	Triumph	Purple
'Orange Emperor'	Fosteriana	Orange
'Oxford'	Darwin Hybrid	Vermilion red
'Purissima'	Fosteriana	White
'Plaisir'	Greigii	Red with white edging
'Red Emperor'	Fosteriana	Red
'Red Riding Hood'	Greigii	Red
'Stresa'	Kaufmanniana	Yellow with red markings
'Striped Apeldoorn'	Darwin Hybrid	Red striped with yellow
T. tarda	Species	Yellow/white
'Toronto'	Greigii	Salmon pink-red
T. turkestanica	Species	White and cream
'Yellow Dover'	Darwin Hybrid	Yellow

LATE BLOOMERS:

'Ballade'	Lily-flowered	Violet with white edges
'Duke of Wellington'	Mayflowered	White
'Maytime'	Lily-flowered	Bright violet, white edges
'West Point'	Lily-flowered	Yellow

THIS PLANTING OF DARWIN HYBRID TULIPS IS A FITTING COMPANION TO THE CIRCULAR BIRDBATH. A BIRD FEEDER HANGS ON THE DOGWOOD NEARBY TO GUARANTEE A STEADY STREAM OF VISITORS AND A LIVELY SHOW.

TO PROTECT BULBS FROM MOLES AND VOLES, SET BULBS IN POTS AND SINK THEM INTO THE
GROUND, OR LINE THE EXCAVATED PLANTING AREA WITH WIRE MESH BEFORE SETTING THE BULBS
IN PLACE.

hyacinths, anemone, *Chionodoxa*, *Eranthis*, *Fritillaria*, *Hyacinthoides*, *Galanthus*, *Muscari*, and *Scilla*. Deer particularly hate *Fritillaria imperialis* became of its strong skunk-like scent; they also don't like thorny plants and avoid perennial astilbes, junipers, foxgloves, ferns, and grasses.

Planting in high-traffic areas close to the house might keep deer and rodents away. Keeping the garden tidy and cleaning up in the fall will also help.

You can also construct barriers to protect your tulip plantings. A deer fence should be at least 7 1/2 feet high; an overhang of chicken wire is a good idea. Since deer can jump something very high or something very wide, but not both at once, a double fence is even more effective. The outside fence should be high, but the inner one can be shorter, about 5 feet high; the two should be spaced about 3 feet apart. (Don't worry, the deer see two fences and don't jump, so they don't get caught inside.)

Garden centers and other retailers also carry various types of plastic fencing and netting that might be appropriate. It is also possible to have an electric anti-deer fence installed. But this isn't recommended for areas where there are small children or close neighbors. For groundhogs, who will eat tulips when they emerge from the ground, and other digging animals, fences don't need to be high, but they do need to be about 3 feet deep.

If the problem is very serious, I most humbly suggest that your best recourse may be to seek only the bulbs listed above that are impervious to animal damage. Or adopt a frisky dog or an army of outdoor cats. They most likely will rectify the problem quickly.

4 Tulips in the Landscape

YOU CAN install a tulip planting virtually anywhere you want in your landscape. Some locations work particularly well:

In flower beds

In flower or shrub borders

Interplanted among foundation plantings

Along driveways, walks, fences, walls, and hedges

In rock gardens

In the middle of ground covers

Naturalized in the lawn or in fields

Beneath spring-flowering trees

Around mailboxes, birdbaths, sundials, or other garden ornaments

Under deciduous trees

In containers on patios or terraces

In a dooryard garden

Of course, if you are going to invest time and money in a tulip planting, you will want it to be in harmony with your landscape and add beauty to your home and surroundings. Although rules are made to be broken, here are a few basics to help you enhance your property.

Always plant at least twelve of the tall tulips (Emperor, Triumph, Darwin Hybrid, Peony, Viridiflora, Parrot, Rembrandt, and Darwin) together, preferably all the same color. It is best to plant twenty-four if your budget and space permit. Low-growing Species tulips should be planted in groups of no less than fifty, but preferably one hundred, or they too will be lost. Greigii and Kaufmanniana tulips should be planted in groups of at least twenty-four, but preferably fifty.

Never buy a rainbow mixture of tulips. The result at bloom time will be a hodgepodge of color, ineffective and often messy looking.

Avoid planting in a straight line or in a single circle around a tree or bush, for the result will look ridiculous and unnatural.

IF YOU HAVE THE SPACE, THERE IS NO BETTER WAY TO SHOWCASE A FAVORITE TREE THAN TO INSTALL A MASS PLANTING OF BULBS AROUND IT. HERE HOT COLORS ARE USED. REDS STAND OUT IN THE BACKGROUND BEST, DRAWING THE EYE.

Concentrate on having two or three colors in each location, and do not mix them. For example, a cluster or drift of violet-colored tulips next to a drift of yellow and a drift of white tulips looks more harmonious than one cluster of each.

Decide whether you want a formal or informal tulip garden and then stick to your decision. Keep in mind that an informal garden is asymmetrical and is thus more appropriate for the majority of residences. Few of us live in houses so stately that a formal planting is called for.

Remember that tall-growing Darwin, Lily-flowered, Triumph, and Darwin Hybrid tulips are stately and somewhat rigid in appearance, so use them sparingly unless you want a very formal look. Species, Greigii, and Kaufmanniana tulips, as well as the taller Peony, Viridiflora, Fringed, Multi-flowered, Parrot, and Rembrandt tulips are often better suited to an informal planting.

Consider the landscape not only from the outdoor point of view, but from indoors as well. Since Species tulips begin blooming in late winter, plant them where you can enjoy them from the comfort of your warm home.

For displays in distant parts of your property, plant large groups of a single variety of tulips in drifts rather than in symmetrical beds. The effect is more natural looking and creates an eye-catching display.

Look at the information on tulip sequence in Chapter 2 to ascertain which tulip bulbs bloom when, and plan your plantings so that you have a sequence of bloom. Be aware that you can interplant and overplant bulbs to enhance a display. (See "Planning Your Tulip Planting" below). Do not use mail-order catalogues to help you choose the varieties for overplanting and interplanting. They often include beautiful photographs of a collection of tulips and other bulbs all in bloom at the same time. These photos are misleading; to create them, the growers force some later-blooming varieties to bloom early. All tulips do not bloom at the same time and you should plan accordingly.

And beware of bargains! Tulips are quite inexpensive in the first place, and bargain collections may include bulbs of inferior quality. As a rule, with almost all planting stock, you get what you pay for. The one exception is the end-of-season sales at nurseries and garden centers. Don't avail yourself of these bargains when installing your bed, as the selection is usually quite limited, but consider buying some inexpensive bulbs this way to fill in your landscape several years later.

PLANNING YOUR TULIP PLANTING

Always design any planting on graph paper. It is usually divided into large blocks, 1 inch square, each of which is further divided into smaller squares, usually six to an inch. Using the scale of one small block to 2 inches of garden space (one large block on the paper will be equal to a square foot in the garden), sketch out the area you wish to plant. This method will not only assure that you purchase enough tulips for your planting, but that you will have a record come fall of exactly where you installed the tulip planting. This will come in handy in the likely event that you will want to fill in a bare area with annuals or interplant and overplant with perennials.

Another way to keep track is to insert markers (plastic or metal)—available at garden centers, nurseries, or through mail-order sources—in place in the garden. Cheap plastic forks work well too. Be sure to label them with an indelible ink pen or a soft-lead pencil.

Alternatively, use oil-based enamels to paint the tops of large aluminum nails—those used for installing rain gutters on houses—in different colors, coded for your plantings, and sink them into the ground in the appropriate places. These are relatively inconspicuous.

In any event, do not trust your memory. While you may think you will remember what is what and what is where, you probably won't.

HERE ARE a few pointers to help you plan your garden:

Tall-growing tulip varieties are generally best placed to the rear of the bed, with medium-height and shorter varieties to the front.

Although it would seem to be obvious, few but the most experienced gardeners are aware of the aesthetic advantages of interplanting and overplanting tulips. By doing so, you can enjoy continuous tulip bloom throughout the spring and summer season. In both cases, first prepare the soil and follow planting instructions and fertilizing instructions in the preceding chapter.

To interplant, select two varieties of tulips or other bulbs that require the same planting depth (check the packages for the depth requirement). Then, simply alternate them within any area, placing them about 2 inches apart. When finished, fill the hole to soil level and water thoroughly.

At Virginia House, in Richmond, Virginia, a planting of pink 'Angelique' Peony tulips underplanted with blue forget-me-nots and set off by the pale pinks of English daisies looks like a pastel-colored cloud. Opposite: By removing bricks from our patio, we accommodated this lovely planting of tulips overplanted with crocuses and snowdrops.

To overplant, plant early-blooming tulips, which require a shallow planting depth, right on top of later-blooming varieties, which require slightly deeper planting. When finished, fill the hole to soil level and water thoroughly.

Variety and contrast are extremely important. Tulips by themselves are classically beautiful but they seem even more magnificent with little grape hyacinths and other minor bulbs playing at their feet.

The tendency of most novice gardeners is to go through catalogues, selecting plants for their beautiful blossoms; they ignore the overall effect they wish to create. Better to strive for a harmonious bed, with colors that blend rather than clash. Plan ahead and then stick to your plan.

White is essential to break up color patterns. At least one-fourth of your tulip planting should be white.

Always think about the color, texture, and shape of the foliage when you select perennials or annuals to plant with your tulips. If a certain cultivar sports a beautiful flower but its foliage is ugly, avoid it. Remember that most plants bear flowers for only a short period, while foliage, with a few exceptions, is present during the entire season. Some perennials are evergreen and add interest to your border or bed during the winter and early spring months, when the first tulips bloom.

When you plant, take your chart to the garden to guide you. Avoid last-minute changes, for they are almost always bad ideas.

COLOR IN YOUR GARDEN

Much has been written about planning a garden that is harmonious in color. I'll include some basic information here, to help you get started.

The color wheel consists of the three primary colors—red, blue, and yellow—and the three secondary colors—purple, green, and orange. Use the color wheel to help plan the color scheme of your garden. Keep in mind that when a color is specified, that means all shades of that color; "red," for example, means pink, carmine, scarlet, etc. And remember

THE SOFT PINK PASTEL OF 'ANGELIQUE' TULIPS IS COMPLEMENTED EQUALLY EFFECTIVELY BY THE DEEPER TONES OF 'SCOTCH LASSIE' (ABOVE) AND THE CONTRASTING SHAPE OF THE LILY-FLOWERED TULIP 'WEST POINT.'

that at least one-fourth of the planting should be white.

Once you've selected your main color (let's say it's purple), concentrate on also using the adjacent colors on the wheel—that is, blue and red of all shades—along with white. An occasional accent can be provided by the opposite color on the wheel—on this case, yellow, either pale or bright. If you select yellow as your main color, concentrate on using the adjacent orange and green along with white; in this case, purple can provide an occasional accent. And so on.

And always keep in mind that all rules are made to be broken.

EFFECTIVE COLOR COMBINATIONS

These combinations of colors work especially well.

BLUE AND YELLOW: Color casts can range from pale yellow to deep gold, sky blue to turquoise. These pairings are used to best advantage when one color is the principal shade and the other is used for accent. Interplant deep-blue grape hyacinths for a rich carpet of blue upon which to show off sulfur-yellow 'Monte Carlo,' a Double Early Tulip.

PINK AND PURPLE: Peony-flowered 'Lilac Perfection' look lovely with perennial pink astilbe or an annual such as a delicate pink forget-me-not. Deep velvety purple or maroon pansies make a good accent.

APRICOT AND PINK: Soft coral tones of 'Apricot Beauty' combine well with the soft pink of 'Peach Blossom' double-flowered tulips.

ROSE, WHITE, AND SALMON: 'Gander's Rhapsody,' a Single Late tulip, is lovely, with its bluish-white cupped blossom blushed with melting rosy hues. Pair it with the pale salmon-pink hyacinth 'Lady Derby.'

YELLOW AND RED: Plant drifts of 'Carioca' Greigii tulips with their brilliant yellow blossoms and carmine-red outer petal markings.

RED AND WHITE: Interplant brilliant red Greigii 'Red Riding Hood' with white patches of daisy-like 'Bridesmaid' *Anemone blanda*.

PURE WHITE: Group 'White Pearl' hyacinths with a drift of pristine 'Purissima,' a white Fosteriana tulip.

ROSE, WHITE, AND YELLOW: For an elegant touch, mix clusters of tall rose-hued 'Mariette' Lily-flowered tulips with pure white 'White Triumphator' Lily-flowered tulips and 'Blushing Beauty,' a velvety yellow-and-apricot Lily-flowered tulip.

YELLOW AND PURPLE: Bright yellow 'West Point,' a Lily-flowered tulip, looks especially striking against a backdrop of purple or orchid azaleas.

ORANGE, PINK, AND SALMON: Flame-colored 'Orange Emperor' Fosteriana tulips and creamy salmon-orange 'Gypsy Queen' hyacinths are stunning when offset by pink daisy-like 'Charmer' *Anemone blanda.* Salmon-pink 'Apricot Beauty,' a Single Early tulip, adds a shimmering touch.

CORAL AND WHITE AND PINK: 'General de Wet,' a delicate coral-orange Single Early tulip is eye-catching with silvery-white 'Pax,' a Triumph tulip, and pink 'Pink Pearl' hyacinths.

PURPLE AND YELLOW: Combine purple, yellow, and white crocuses with 'Lilac Wonder' Species tulips. Deep purple or burgundy tulips are stunning in front of lime-yellow, bushy euphorbia.

PURPLE OR BLUE AND BRIGHT RED: A large drift of 'Blue Giant' *Scilla hispanica* overplanted with white and magenta 'Sorbet' Single Late tulips is very effective. Another blue-red combo is *Iris reticulata* with early-blooming vermilion-red *T. praestans* 'Fusilier.'

MAGENTA AND BLUE: Magenta 'Electra,' a Double Early tulip, with deep purple or violet-blue companion plantings of pansies or 'Blue Magic' hyacinths is stunning.

COMPLEMENTING EARLY-BLOOMING TULIP PLANTINGS

You usually cannot complement an early spring blooming tulip garden with annuals, because most annuals are tender and will not tolerate late frosts. However, biennial pansy plants, usually available at garden centers in late March in six-packs, are frost resistant and will thrive in the cold. They are available in a wide range of colors, and particularly complement low-growing early tulips. But many other bulbs and perennials can be used in tandem with tulip plantings.

Early-blooming bulbs other than tulips can be interplanted and overplanted with early-blooming tulips. You can add various "minor" bulbs to these plantings.

PLANT	DESCRIPTION
Anemone 'de Caen'	Red, white, pink, blue, purple
Bulbocodium vernum	Pale lavender
Crocus, Dutch	Gold, blue, white, purple, silver
Crocus, Species	White, cream, yellow, purple, blue, lilac
Daffodil, Miniature	Yellow, white, gold. 'February Gold' is the earliest.
Eranthis (Winter aconite)	Buttercup shaped; yellow
Galanthus (Snowdrop)	White
Iris danfordiae	Brilliant yellow
Iris reticulata	Purple, white, pale blue, lilac

IF YOU ARE LOOKING TO MAKE A STATEMENT, EARLY-BLOOMING KAUFMANNIANA 'SHAKESPEARE' TULIPS ALONG WITH BLUE DUTCH CROCUSES WILL CERTAINLY FIT THE BILL.

These early-blooming perennials, all appropriate tulip companions, work especially well in a rock garden or low-growing border area, and almost all bloom in tandem with early Species, Fosteriana, Kaufmanniana, Greigii, Single Early, and mid-season Darwin Hybrids and Triumph tulips.

PLANT	DESCRIPTION
Aethionema x warleyense (Warley Rose)	Pink
Alyssum saxatile	Brilliant sulfur yellow
Alyssum 'Citrum'	Pale yellow
Alyssum 'Sunny Border Apricot'	Apricot
Anemone pulsatilla	White, red, or purple; bell-shaped
Arabis	Mounds of clusters of white
Armeria (Thrift)	Deep rose; pincushion-shaped
Asperula (Sweet woodruff)	Small; white
Aubrieta (Rock cress)	Mounds of purple, blue, or white
Brunnera macrophylla	Blue
Dicentra eximia	Pink; pantaloon-shaped
Doronicum	Bright yellow; daisy-shaped
Draba sibirica	Tiny; yellow
Echiveria (Hens and chicks)	Succulent foliage of pink, green, jade, purple, red
Helleborus orientalis (Lenten rose)	Pink
Iberis (Candytuft)	Clusters of white
Lamium maculatum	Clusters of white
Mertensia virginica	Blue; bell-shaped
Primula	Yellow, rust, red, pink, blue, purple
Pulmonaria angustifolia	Yellow
Pulmonaria 'Mrs. Moon'	Small blue blossoms
Sedum	Yellow, pink, white; small
Stachys byzantina (Lamb's ears)	Silver foliage
Trillium grandiflorum	Large white blossoms
Viola	Blue, apricot, yellow, purple, white

COMPLEMENTING MID-SEASON AND LATE-BLOOMING TULIP PLANTINGS

As the season progresses, more and more bulbs and perennials flower. These can used to great advantage in planning a garden containing mid-season to Mayflowering tulips. The following bulbs all bloom in March and April, with some still blooming in May in most parts of the country.

PLANT	DESCRIPTION
Anemone blanda	White, blue, pink, purple daisy-like blooms
Allium	Many different colors and heights
Camassia	Feathery blue spikes
Chionodoxa (Glory-of-the-snow)	Blue with white eye
Convallaria (Lily-of-the-valley)	White; bell-shaped
Daffodil	Yellow, white, orange, pink
Erythronium (Japanese pagoda)	Yellow, white, pink
Fritillaria imperialis	Red, orange, or yellow
Fritillaria meleagris	Purple and white or white
~~*Fritillaria michailovskyi*~~	~~Bronze and yellow~~
Hyacinth, Dutch	Pink, purple, blue, red, rose, white, yellow, or apricot
Ipheion	White
Iris, Dutch	Yellow, blue, purple, bronze, white
Iris, Miniature and Dwarf	All colors of the rainbow
Leucojum (Snowflake)	White
Muscari (Grape hyacinth)	Deep blue, light blue, or white
Ornithogalum umbellatum	White and pale green
Puschkinia (Lebanon squill)	Pale blue
Scilla hispanica (Spanish bluebells)	White, blue, pink
Scilla siberica (Squill)	Bright, electric blue, pale blue, or white

All perennials can be planted in the fall when you install the bulbs or, if need be, in the spring. If you wish to overplant early-blooming bulbs with perennials, it is best to plant both in the fall. Many perennials bloom in May and are suitable for combining with Mayflowering tulips.

PLANT	DESCRIPTION
Achillea (Yarrow)	Sulfur yellow, pale yellow, rose, white or lavender
Ajuga (Bugleweed)	Deep blue; spikes
Anthemis (Golden marguerite)	Bright yellow; daisy-shaped
Aquilegia (Columbine)	All colors
Arenaria (Sandwort)	Mats of white
Centaurea montana (Cornflower)	Deep blue
Dianthus (Pinks)	Many shades of red, pink, salmon, white
Dicentra (Bleeding heart)	Pink or white
Geranium (Cranesbill)	Blue, pink, magenta, white
Geum	Orange, yellow, crimson, pink
Heuchera (Coral bells)	Pink, red, white
Iris, German	All colors
Myosotis (Forget-me-not)	Tiny blue blossoms
Peony	Red, pink, yellow, white
Phlox divaricata (Wild phlox)	Blue
Phlox stolonifera (Creeping phlox)	Blue, red, pink, white
Phlox subulata (Moss pinks)	Blue, red, pink, white
Polemonium (Jacob's ladder)	Blue
Polygonatum (Solomon's seal)	Creamy white
Saponaria (Soapwort)	Pink mats
Trollius (Globeflower)	Bright yellow
Veronica prostrata (Speedwell)	Blue; matlike

COMPLEMENTING EXISTING SHRUBS
AND FLOWERING TREES

Keep in mind that many shrubs and spring-flowering trees can be
complemented with tulip plantings. White, pink, or deep-rose dogwoods
underplanted with pink, white, and pale-yellow Mayflowering tulips are
stunning. During the spring blooming season, I move thistle feeders
from tree to tree as they bloom. Goldfinches, who relish thistle, decorate
the trees with their brilliant yellow plumage. Beneath are plantings of
various colored tulips. Needless to say, the effect is breathtaking.

Lilacs are in bloom at this time and combine well with purple, white,

86

PINK LILY-FLOWERED TULIP 'JACQUELINE' COUPLED WITH OLD-FASHIONED BLEEDING HEART
(DICENTRA SPECTABILIS) SWEETLY ANNOUNCES SPRING WITH ITS SOFT COLOR.

yellow, pink, and rose tulips, along with deep-blue *Muscari*. Flowering peach, apricot, and apple trees all sport pink or white blossoms and also set off a tulip planting. The deep red of hawthorne looks sensational with brilliant red and yellow late-blooming *Stellata magnolia* and *Soulangeiana*. Magnolia's white, yellow, pink, or purple bloom can be enhanced by tall Mayflowering tulips.

Azaleas, rhododendrons, Korean rhododendrons, forsythia, spirea, flowering quince, flowering almond, and many other flowering shrubs also bloom at this time of year and work beautifully with tulip plantings.

OUTDOOR CONTAINERS

Container tulips add a lovely dimension to any garden. Use them to grace your front entryway or line your walks. Or place them on decks and terraces for a spring show, so that you can sit and enjoy them on balmy days. They are also perfect accents for courtyards, balconies, and flat rooftops and along driveways, window ledges, fire escapes, and retaining walls. Use them for camouflaging unattractive storage sheds or garbage cans. Some gardeners prefer a unified look with one type or color of flower such as a terra-cotta pot of Single Early 'Apricot Beauty' tulips or a shallow stone planter of Peony-flowering 'Angelique.' Others like to combine tulips with early-blooming pansies for a multicolor, mini-garden effect.

Start by planting your containers as instructed for forcing (see Chapter 5). Then put containers outdoors in a place sheltered from the wind and (in the North) extreme cold or (in the South) hot sun. Outdoor containers should be a minimum of 14 inches across to withstand overwintering outdoors. In extremely cold climates, put containers in an unheated, protected area like a garage or shed. If a container is too heavy to move, wrap it with newspaper and burlap. In the South, keep pots cool, out of the sun, and preferably with a northern exposure. And avoid dark containers, which trap heat.

Water the containers over the winter. Aside from being essential for growing, water also protects the bulbs from frost injury. Keep containers moist, but not soggy. Mulch will help retain moisture.

With containers planted and positioned for the winter, and fall planting directly in the ground all behind you, sit back and wait for spring, knowing that your garden will be more beautiful than ever before.

5 Tulips Indoors

A FEW EASY steps will ensure that your flower arrangements will be as beautiful and long-lasting as possible.

CUTTING TULIPS

WHEN TO CUT

The best time to cut tulips is early in the morning, while the dew is still on the blossoms. This means that they will have had the long, cool night to revive after the warmth of the previous day. If this is impossible, cut at sunset. Never cut during the heat of the day—because the sun's heat causes the moisture in the blossoms and foliage to evaporate, leaving them somewhat stressed.

HOW TO CUT AND CONDITION TULIPS

Select buds with color on top and green on the bottom. If a bud is tightly closed and all green, with no flower color showing, it won't open.

Never pull or break flower stems by hand. Always cut with a sharp knife or scissors at a 45-degree angle. This will expose a larger area of the cut stem to water, facilitating greater absorption than a cut made straight across. To save stress on the cuttings, immediately place them in a large pail filled with air-temperature water, immersing the stems.

When you have cut enough tulips for an arrangement, take the pail to a work area indoors. One by one, place each cutting in a container with 6 inches of room-temperature water. Holding the bottom of the stem underwater, cut off an inch or so of the stem at a 45-degree angle. Remove all leaves that will ultimately be beneath the water line. Wrap the entire bouquet in a chimney of oaktag or stiff paper and reimmerse it in a pailful of room-temperature water. Mist the flower heads with water. Leave overnight.

TULIP ARRANGEMENTS LOOK LOVELY IN ANY KIND OF CONTAINER. TO MAKE THE FLOWERS LAST LONGER, CUT THE STEMS AND CHANGE THE WATER FREQUENTLY. THAT'S ALL.

Arranging the Flowers

Tulips look at home in any type of container, from the homeliest tin to the prettiest crystal vase. When you are ready to arrange them, remember that most flowers like cut-flower food in the water, but tulips are the exception. They prefer their water straight. To keep them fresh and vigorous, top the container off with fresh cold water every day or so, or change the water daily for longest vase life. With proper care, tulip buds will open in the first few days in the vase and last a week or more. For longest life, keep bouquets in a cool spot, away from sources of heat such as radiators and television sets, and recut the stem ends every day or two.

Unlike most cut flowers, tulips keep growing in the vase. And, as they grow taller, often an inch or more, they tend to bend toward sources of light. Most people enjoy the unpredictable twists and turns of tulips, but if you wish to straighten the stems, simply remove the flowers from the vase, trim the stems, and roll the tulips in newspaper with the paper extending above the flower tops but not covering the lower third of the stems. Place the wrapped bunch upright in a container holding enough cool water to submerge the exposed stems. Leave in a cool place for an hour or two. Your tulips will then stand tall, and you can return them to the vase.

And please! No pennies in the water for your tulips. Such ideas often persist long after scientific evidence proves them wrong. Home remedies abound for keeping cut tulips fresh longer in the vase. Add pennies, they say, or aspirin, bleach, or even diluted 7 UP! But the fact is that tulips thrive on just plain clean water. While each of these home remedies provides some "quick fix" benefits, none is actually the best additive for cut flowers, and certainly not for tulips. "Tulips are self-sufficient," says Frans Roozen, technical director of the International Flower Bulb Center, in Hillegom, Holland. The home remedies keep circulating, he says, "because people use them, see immediate results with their own eyes and say, 'Yes it is true!' But what they see is merely a mini-surge of energy in the flower and not the aftermath, which is often a shortened life span."

The Best Varieties for Cutting

The Netherlands Flowerbulb Institute says these tulips are known for especially long vase life, often up to two weeks: 'Angelique,' 'Attila,' 'Don Quichotte,' 'Ile de France,' 'Leen van der Mark,' 'Negrita,' 'Pax,' 'Princess

Irene,' 'Queen of Bartignons,' 'Rosario,' and 'Yokohama.' Almost all other tulips will stay fresh in the vase for at least one week, if conditioned as above.

FORCING TULIPS

Each year, in late winter or early spring—long before tulips bloom outdoors—you've probably noticed pots of blooming tulips and other bulbs for sale at garden centers, nurseries, florist shops, and even supermarkets. These bulbs were forced, and it's quite easy to do. You can do it at home by following these simple instructions. Just think of the joy of having your house filled with cheerful blooming tulips in February and March.

SELECTING CONTAINERS

Although you can grow tulip bulbs in just about any kind of container imaginable, the traditional bulb pan of clay or plastic is probably the best because the essential drainage holes are provided. As a rule, the pot should be about twice as deep as the height of a bulb. In other words, a tulip bulb that measures 2 inches from top to bottom should be potted in a 4-inch-deep pot.

CONDITIONING CONTAINERS

Some containers have to be conditioned before planting. Soak brand-new terra-cotta or clay containers in water overnight so they will not absorb the water necessary for the planting medium. Soak used terra-cotta, clay, or plastic containers overnight in a solution of one part household bleach to three parts water to kill any disease organism that might be on the surface. New plastic containers need no conditioning.

SOIL MIXTURE

Use a soil mixture, such as Redi-Earth or Terra-lite, that is recommended for starting seedlings. Potting soil is not good, as it is usually too heavy. If you wish to make your own soil mix, combine equal amounts of packaged potting soil, sphagnum peat moss (wet and then squeezed until almost dry), and horticultural or builder's sand. Add 1 cup perlite or horticultural vermiculite to each quart of soil mix.

PLANTING

First, cover the drainage holes in the bottoms of the pots with pebbles, rocks, broken flowerpot shards, or the white plastic "popcorn" used by mail-order houses to pack merchandise. Then fill the pot about two-thirds full with soil mix. Set a bulb so its top is half an inch below the rim of the pot. Adjust the soil level if necessary. Set more bulbs on the soil, making sure they do not touch. Fill the pot with soil mix. Do not pack it; bulb roots require loosely packed soil to grow properly.

Take special care when you place the bulbs in the pot. The first leaves that tulip bulbs produce grow from the flat side of the bulb, so place the flat sides closer to the outside of the pot. This will make the ultimate effect more aesthetically pleasing, with the large leaves serving as an outer display of foliage.

Water the pots thoroughly. Fill in cavities with more soil mix if necessary. Be sure to label each pot, so that when it comes time to force bloom you will know which is which.

THE CHILLING PROCESS

For tulip bulbs to bloom before their normal time, they need a cool environment, just as they require below-freezing temperatures when they are planted in the garden. There are three different ways to do this.

First, you can sink pots into a cold frame outdoors, covering with a 6–8-inch layer of salt hay or sand. You'll have to make trips out to the garden in the dead of winter to see if the bulb shoots are emerging, and it is often difficult in very cold weather to remove the protective covering because it is frozen stiff or covered with ice and snow. However, if you have no other option, this is the way to do it.

The second way, which is much easier and equally as effective, is to place the pots in the cellar or in an unheated garage. The temperature ideally should stay between 30 and 50 degrees. Cover pots with newspaper so that no light falls on the bulbs. They will need to be watered approximately every four weeks. Even so, it is a good idea to check the soil every week; if it is dry to the touch, water moderately. Good root growth is essential for successful forcing.

The third method is to chill in a refrigerator. Place the potted bulbs inside and check every now and then to see if watering is necessary. Never place pots in the freezer!

Forcing Bloom

After the cooling period, when light yellow-green shoots have emerged and are about 2–3 inches high, it is time to bring the pots into warmer temperatures. Place the pots in a cool indoor location, either in darkness or in bright, indirect sunlight, for three to five weeks.

During this period, bulbs will develop strong top growth. Check soil occasionally and water if necessary. As soon as flower buds appear, place pots in a location with cool temperatures (50–60°F) and direct sunlight. Once the buds begin to show color—after ten days to two weeks—the pots can be moved wherever they will be admired. Keep in mind that the cooler the temperature, especially at night, the longer the bulbs will stay in bloom. Under optimum conditions, plants displayed in an area no warmer than 65°F should stay in bloom for a week to ten days.

It is best to dispose of forced tulips after they bloom, as they usually do not bloom again when planted in the ground.

Tulip bulbs are planted with their pointed side up and can be grown successfully in almost any kind of container, as long as drainage holes are provided. Force them indoors to enjoy them in the bleak days of late winter.

TIMING

If you want to have bulbs in bloom on a particular date—Easter, for example—keep in mind that rooting takes twelve to fourteen weeks, and forcing takes approximately ten days to two weeks. So, from planting to flowering, the whole process takes from fourteen to sixteen weeks.

THE BEST TULIPS FOR FORCING

Many tulips are easy to force, but these are particularly successful: 'Angelique,' 'Barcelona,' 'Cassini,' 'Debutante,' 'Madison Garden,' 'Monte Carlo,' 'Negrita,' 'Orange Cassini,' 'Pinocchio,' and 'Plaisir.'

JUST THE THING TO CURE A CASE OF THE LATE-WINTER BLUES—A COLORFUL DISPLAY OF FORCED TULIPS AND DAFFODILS.

SOURCES

IN JUNE or July, it is a good idea to request catalogues from these mail-order tulip sources. Almost all the catalogues are beautifully illustrated with full-color photographs that will help you make your selections.

BRENT AND BECKY'S BULBS
7463 Heath Trail
Gloucester, VA 23061
(877) 661-2852
www.brentandbeckysbulbs.com

MCCLURE & ZIMMERMAN
108 W. Winnebago St.
P.O. Box 368
Friesland, WI 53935-0368
(800) 883-6998
www.mzbulb.com

PARK SEED COMPANY
1 Parkton Avenue
Greenwood, SC 29647-0001
(800) 845-3369
www.parkseed.com

JOHN SCHEEPERS
23 Tulip Drive
Bantam, CT 06750-1631
(860) 567-0838
www.johnscheepers.com

VAN BOURGONDIEN
245 Route 109
P.O. Box 1000
Babylon, NY 11702-9004
(800) 622-9997
www.dutchbulbs.com

WAYSIDE GARDENS
1 Garden Lane
Hodges, SC 29695-0001
(800) 845-1124
www.waysidegardens.com

WHITE FLOWER FARM
P.O. Box 50
Litchfield, CT 06759-0050
(800) 503-9624
www.whiteflowerfarm.com

INDEX